Say It's the Sea

Kristina Mahr

Still for you.

What if today I'm not afraid.
Just one day of courage.
Of bold moves & irrefutable hope.
Just one day of vulnerability.
Of my heart put out into the world,
small & scarred & pulsing.
Just one day of saying yes when I want to say yes
& no when I want to say no.
Of not even needing to give a reason other than
"it's what my heart wants."
What if today I'm not afraid.

And then today becomes tomorrow
becomes the day after
becomes the whole rest of my life.

KRISTINA MAHR

Only the One

I have only the one heart, and
I gave it to only the one person.

That he is gone now
doesn't change
these facts.

Fall Back

I will use this extra hour as
I have used the ones before, as I
will use the ones that come after—
if you were here, it would be
loving you; with you gone, it is
only
     missing you.

On My Way

This is the least lost
I've ever been, though
I've never been here
before, though I have
no idea where I am,
though I do not know
my way out.

Amid so much that I
don't know, I know
that I'm on my way
to you.

Unknow

I would never wish
to unknow you, but
I would wish to unknow
the version of you
that no longer loves me.

Everything

Everything hurts. (That's no way
to start a poem.) My heart hurts.
(That's better.) But let's think about
anatomy. About blood sent coursing
through veins with every pump,
pulse, pound, with every shudder, shift,
shatter. Blood to my head and blood
to my toes. Who says it's only
blood. Who says nothing else could
stow away, could spread, could sweep
from head to toe and back again.

What I'm saying is everything hurts.

(But you can trace it all back to the heart.)

Thank You

When I say good morning, I mean
thank you for being here when I wake up.

When I say goodnight, I mean
thank you for falling asleep beside me.

When I say I'm sorry, I mean
thank you for listening to me try to explain.

When I say I miss you, I mean
thank you for being mine to miss.

When I say I love you, I mean
thank you for being the person you are.

And every inhale, every exhale, carries
on the back of it a
thank you for loving me.

For You

This is a poem that I
don't want to write. I will
probably call it something like
For You, and it won't rhyme.
I will be both sorry and glad
when other people tell me
they relate to it. I will hope that
you read it. I will hope that you
don't read it. I will try to find a
way to sneak in the words *I
love you*, maybe the words
I miss you, probably the words
come back. It will be hard to call it
poetry. I will reread it half a dozen
times, but it will never become just
words, just letters, just a piece of paper.

It will always be something like
bravery, something like my heart.

It will always be for you.

Shambles

He says
I have a beautiful
smile, and I say
thank you, when what
I really want to
say is, can you tell
that everything behind it
is in shambles.

December

This is how it is— nobody wants to
hear me say that it's December now.

Nobody wants to hear me say
it, and I don't want to say it, but you
and I both know that what I want
has never really mattered.

It's December now.

It would be December even if
I didn't say it.

And you'd still be gone.

Do You

One foot in front of
the other, do you
hear me.

Are my eyes
open. (Then why
can't I see you.) Are
my ears uncovered.
(Then why can't I
hear you.) Do you
still love me. (Then
why can't I feel you.)

One foot in front of
the other, do you
hear me.

Do you, can you, will you.

Looking

Maybe I've been doing this
all wrong, looking for you instead
of looking for love.

So now I look for love.

(I still hope to find you.)

Scared

And I'm scared that there will come a time
when I am sad and don't think to call you.

And I'm scared that there will come a time
when I am happy and don't think to call you.

But mostly I'm scared that there will come a time
when I think to call you and you

don't answer.

A Choice

I have a choice— believe the best
in you or believe the worst.

(I let my heart decide.)

Kindling

We've always made good
kindling; I've just always preferred
the way we burn together
over the way
I burn
here
without you.

A Sign

I ask the universe for
a sign as though
the fact that you're not here

isn't

one.

A Wandering

I have a wandering inside of me, a bit of
lostness inside of me, a little *come find me,
come find me, come find me* inside of
me, pure catastrophe inside of me, truly
chaos inside of me, you say reckless and
I say just restless inside of me, I have a
wanting inside of me, so much reaching
inside of me, on the tips of my toes and
a leaning inside of me, do you look deep
inside of me, do you see deep inside of
me, do you want to know just what I
hold deep inside of me—

echoes, your name, and my heart.

echoes, your name, and my heart.

Mistaken

I'm sorry, I've mistaken you
for somebody else, I say, to
strangers on the street I
chase after when they have
your laugh and to you
when you tell me
you don't love me anymore.

Nobody Fought

This did not end with
fire; not with drowning;
nobody screamed, nobody
yelled, nobody

fought.

It ended with silence.

(I would have preferred the fire.)

To Feel Alive

Some people need to
jump out of planes
to feel alive; I just need
to love you.

Hell If

I don't need you.

But hell if I don't
want you badly enough
to make it feel like
I do.

A Tendency

I keep
an eye
on hope—

it has
a tendency
to get

lost.

Wake Me Up

You are
the opposite of
a lullaby; you are
the song I sing
when I need
to wake up.

I Can Swim

You are so sure I'll drown,
you've never given me the chance
to show you how well
I can swim.

In My Bones

I carry winter in my bones, tucked in beside
you. My hands shake and my heart is a
hearth. Something is dying inside me. Something
is living inside me. One does not cancel out
the other. I do not want them to.

You know, I thought I might love you less by now.

Two Months

I keep running around
the kitchen island, and you
keep chasing me, and we
are laughing, and
I never let you catch me, I
never let you catch me, because
if I do, two months will pass and
you won't love me anymore.

Blue

I answer the phone, though it wasn't
ringing. I open the door, though no
one knocked. It is quiet in here, silent
in here, though I am calling your
name. Maybe I am wrong, it occurs
to me I may be wrong. I have turned
my back on air because I think I can
breathe hope. In the mirror, I see
I am turning blue.

Your favorite color, I think, as I call
your name one more time.

This Christmas

Last Christmas, all I asked for
was your heart.

This Christmas, all I asked for
was mine back.

What Am I

What am I?

A girl, a risk,
a mess of words
and wants.

In love with you.

Maybe Mars

Maybe Mars just had its heart broken.
We declare no sign of life, and we do not
hear it say, *I'm trying, I'm trying.* We say it's
cold up there, it's dark up there, and we do not
hear it say, *I didn't use to be this way.* We look around
a bit and go, and we do not
hear it say,

please don't leave me here alone.

Everywhere

How beautiful
to miss someone
who is everywhere
I look.

This Tinder Heart

I am less afraid
of this tinder heart
now that I've seen
what I can pull
from its ashes.

Hot Potato

We play hot potato with
my heart; neither of us
wants to be holding it when
it breaks.

The irony is, I think this
will be the thing
that breaks it.

To Have To

It isn't difficult
to miss you, no;

it's difficult to have to.

No Closer

I say I'm sorry to
who I'll be tomorrow—

who I am today did not
get any closer to
not loving you.

The Answer

If love is not the answer,
then I am fairly certain
I will never understand
the question.

Inches or Miles

I never know
if you are inches or miles
from taking my hand,
but I keep it held out
for you.

Midnight

What do you know,
the clock struck midnight and
I still loved you.

Forgive Me

Forgive me for how
I treated your heart
when I did not know
I had it.

How Many Stars

Do you remember when
we loved each other? I wonder
how many stars
have died
since then.

Never Going to Be

I am not ashamed of my knees
when they buckle / and I am not
ashamed of my fists when they
clench / and I am not ashamed of
my tongue when it ties / and I am
not ashamed of my eyes when
they drip / and I am not / and I am
not / and I am never going to be

ashamed of my heart

when it keeps

loving you.

Yellow Light

You are a light that has just
turned yellow, and I speed up
like I can make it, like I stand
a chance, like I don't know
exactly what
comes
next.

Wide as the World

I am trying to open my
arms as wide as the world
because I don't know which
part of it you might be in
or if you might need me.

Stitches

I've been so proud of how
I stitched my heart back together
that it took me til now to realize—

the stitches spell your name.

Less

I saw a movie today, and for
the first time in a long time,
my hand did not feel empty
without yours in it. I do not
think I'd call that loving you
less; I think I'd call that
starting to forgive you
for loving me less.

Quicksand

They say to keep your hands free.

They say to make yourself as light
as possible, try to back up, reach,
reach, reach. Reach for anything that
might save you. Breathe in, breathe
out. Breathe in, breathe out. They
say stay calm. Don't panic. Go
slow. Don't panic.

They say to keep your hands free.

Keep them high.

Keep them yours.

Memory Lane

I almost never drive memory lane
sober. I am reckless, a fool, one
hand on the wheel and the other
somewhere in yours. My eyes are
on the rearview mirror, always on
the rearview mirror, only on the
rearview mirror. My heart is in
my throat— no. My heart is on
my sleeve— no. Where did you
put my heart, can you tell me
where you put my heart.

I want you, but you knew that. I miss
you, but you knew that. I love you, but—

I know this road does not really
lead me back to you.

All the Wrong Things

We built goodbye from
bricks, hope from
sticks, love from
straw, and together
we blew all the
wrong things to
the ground.

While You're Here

I don't want to hold you here;

I just want to hold you while you're here.

Afraid

I hid from you
because I was afraid
of you, but I was only
afraid of you because
you hid
from me.

Abracadabra

Look at this, would you
look at this—

I have peeled away the

bitter

and only left the

sweet.

Something Small and Lonely

Lately my body is a house and I am something
small and lonely locked inside of it, trying to hold
it all together, rushing to my hands to pry my
fingers open before realizing that my feet are
carrying me back to you, and as I hurry down to
try to stop them, my lips form the shape of
your name and a *stop* and a *please*, and I cannot
get to them in time, I cannot get to them in time,
and my heart, my heart is breaking and it is
taking down the walls of me, it is taking down
the all of me, and I swear, I swear, I am trying
to hold it all together, but—

I am only something small and lonely.

And your laugh is in here with me.

And I am scared that it will leave me, too.

Lone Survivor

Sometimes I think
at the end of the world,
the only thing left standing
will be my heart with you
inside of it.

Cracked

Heart like a cracked raw egg, spilling
everything soft and willful out into
the world as though it has a chance of
holding me; as though its hands are
something close to gentle; as though
it is not riddled with cracks of its own.

Still, I do not walk lightly upon the shells of it.

I run,

and I do not

look back.

To the Light

I follow my heart
through the darkness
because I trust
it is leading me
to the light.

Silence

Why, of all the things we
made so fragile, did we not
make silence one of them.

Life Lessons

You cannot pour love into a cup
that they have covered with
their hand.

You can try, I mean,
you can try.

But it will leave a mess and you

will have to mop it up

alone.

It Was Still Love

Do not fool yourself into
thinking any of this was
easy. But oh, it was still
love. It was still love. It
was still beautiful.

Only That

I can't remember
the color of your eyes—
only that they
said forever, and
only that they

lied.

It's Complicated

When people ask about us I say
it's complicated, but maybe it isn't.

Maybe I just love you and maybe you

just don't care.

Just Words

These are just words on paper.

And they don't mean I love you.

And they don't mean I don't.

Not Enough

I like to think that
Wendy went off and
built herself a life,
a good life.

And that Peter missed her.

(Just not enough.)

The Sun, the Moon, and You

The sun makes me hope,

the moon makes me dream,

and you, you make

me love.

More

There is a difference between what
you owe me and what I deserve.

Which is to say, you don't owe me
a goddamn thing, but

I think

I deserve

more.

Until We Weren't

What more is there
to say? We were
happy. We were
happy. We were
happy until we

weren't.

A Hollow Victory

I am soft-edged but sharp-
tongued. *I love you* is a challenge
I handed you, and you did not
know how to meet it. It is a hollow
victory that years later still tastes
strongly of defeat.

You have never asked for my
forgiveness, but here, take it,
I don't want it anymore. Put it with
I love you.

Either where you put
the things you care about or
where you put the things you

don't.

The Ocean's Memory

If water has a memory, I wonder if
the ocean thinks we're still
together.

It would only remember us laughing.

It never saw me cry.

Can You Imagine

He says I have his heart, and can you
imagine? Can you imagine? What would
I do with it? Where would I put it? The
blood, imagine the blood, imagine the
mess. Oh, can you imagine, how would
he live? How would the blood pump
through his body, how would he smile
at me with a hole gaping in his chest,
how would he hold me without me
falling headfirst into it? Can you imagine?
I tell him no, I tell him to take it back, I
tell him to keep it. Me, with my small hands,
how would I hold it? Me, with my careless
words, how would I not crush it?

I tell him to take it back.

It's not that I don't want it, no,
it's not that I don't want it.

But I tell him to take it back.

A Complicated Existence

It is a complicated
existence, by which
I mean love is involved,
by which I mean
I would not have it
any other way.

Black Holes

Eyes like black holes, and I

have lost everything in them.

Shattered

Maybe sometimes the ship sees
the rocks. Maybe it could turn around
in time. Maybe it just wants

to get a little bit

shattered.

The First, the Only

You were the first time I ever
jumped in without testing the
water. I had no idea if it was
boiling, if it was freezing. If
my feet could touch the
bottom, if there was any way
for me to climb back out. I had
no idea, I had no idea, I had
no idea, but I jumped, and—

you were the only time

I ever jumped in

without testing

the water.

20/20 Faith

Not blind faith, no. 20/20
faith. A clearing faith. No
rain or snow in the forecast
faith. I have held you faith.
I have touched you faith.
I have loved you faith.

Not blind faith, no.

I know you faith.

About Love

Love, let me tell you about
love, what can I tell you about
love. It is there through bad and
there through sad. There through
rage and there through age. There
through shame and there through
blame. There through pain and
there through rain.

There through dawn and—

there through gone.

Say Something

There is a deer outside my window, what would
you say about this deer. Would you acknowledge
it. Say something about overpopulation. Say
something about natural predators. Say
something about swerving late at night on a
two-lane road so as not to hit one. Say
something about its beauty. Say something
about the way the sun looks setting behind it.
Say something about its loneliness.

The snow was not this deep. This song was not
yet out. I did not know how much I loved you.

And you were never here to see
this deer outside my window.

So I have to imagine
what you'd
say.

Fairy Tales

I bought into
fairy tales to
love you.

Too Much

Maybe this is enough
hurt. You know? Maybe this is
too much hurt
to still be able to call it

love.

What's the Point

My love for you is
a song that has never been
sung— it exists, but what's
the point.

Say It's the Sea

The tide grabs you by
the ankles and drags you
back out to sea every time
you reach for me. Right? Say
it's the tide. Say it's the sea.
Say you are not
choosing this.

Even I

I knew well the depth
of my love for you, but
even I am surprised by
its length.

Burning Burning Burning

What I know of love is that
I am cold to my bones and it
is a whistling tea kettle; I grab
onto it hoping for warmth but it
is burning burning burning and—

I cannot let it go.

Need

I don't use the word need
so much since you; it turns
out we can live with
far less than
we thought.

The Very Best

Me, no, nobody, no,
nobody gets the best
of me, nobody gets
the best of me, I let
nobody get the best
of me.

(Except you.)

I let you have
the very best of me.

These Are the Things We Don't Talk About

closed eyes / reaching hands / May / we don't
talk about May / we never talk about May /
hope / and how it bends / love / and how it
breaks / goodbye / and how it rolls off your
tongue / goodbye / and how it sticks on
mine / words / all of these words / every one
of these words / whether you hear a single one
of these words / what was / what is / what will be /
what could be / what won't be / why / we
don't talk about / why / we never talk about

why not.

(why not?)

This Is the Part

This is the part where you stay.

This is the part where you stay.

This is the part where it's hard

and you stay anyway.

Open Hands

I am trying to live with
open hands; I know
you need to go.

I am trying to live with
open hands.

(That means you can come back.)

Pretend

He likes to pretend
he knows me, and I
like to pretend
I'd ever let him.

Broken

They fixed my car up so well you can't even tell
I crashed it into the back of a pickup truck in the
snow one night, you can't even tell, no, but when
I tried to sell it, they said it's not worth as much
anymore. Even though it looks so good, runs so
good, you can't even tell it was once crushed
so badly I had to climb out the passenger side
door, no, they said it's not worth as much anymore.

The trouble is, nothing can ever be unbroken.

It can be fixed, and it can look so good, run
so good, you can't even tell.

But it can never
not have been
broken.

There Is No Way

I don't know you
anymore, and
there is no way
to turn that into
poetry.

I Call

I call this a poem, but if you
sing it, it's a song. I call these
words, but if you push them
all together, they're a story.
I call you by your name, but
if you come back, it's

love.

Thawed

I see now why
you liked me
frozen— the
second I thawed
I slipped
right through
your fingers.

Imagine It Like This

This is how I say I love you / this /
here / words that are not I / or love /
or you / but are instead something
about stars / maybe something about
a hand / a flower / something opening /
something beautiful / I say it with
my pen / instead of my voice / and you
will never know / how hard I press /
how I tear through / page after page /
you will never know / but imagine
it like this—

if I said it / my voice would /
not shake.

if I said it / my voice / would
not shake.

No More

I have no intention
of taking my love
back. Keep it, it's
yours. You just
won't be getting
any more.

Push/Pull

How dare you say
I am pulling away
when I am fighting
for traction and you

keep

pushing.

A Thousand Miles Away

I don't even stay long enough to
hear you say it. You say *I* and I am
halfway across the room. You say
love and I'm already out the door. You
say *you* and I'm a thousand miles
away, wondering if someday I will
wish I'd tried harder to stay.

Be Brave

What I know of fear
is that it has cost me
far more
than bravery ever has.

Maybe Someday

Maybe someday
this will all
make sense,
but for now
I still love you
too much
to understand.

Trust Fall

Loving you is a trust fall off
a skyscraper. I have been
plummeting for some time
now, and with each passing
second, I am either more or
less sure than ever before
that you will be at the bottom
to catch me.

The Odds

I lose every time I bet
on you, but I still bet on
you every time. I don't bet
small, either, no, I go all in
every time, every single
time. It takes me a while
to recoup what I lost. It takes
me a while, and then I bet it
all on you again.

My heart has never
cared about the odds.

It is too busy
loving you.

Softly Struck

I wish I could say that
it did not come as a
surprise when one
night the realization
softly struck me
that I am no less
worthy of love
just because you
did not love me.

Love Takes

Love takes me out to dinner and
says I look pretty, so pretty. Love
takes the long way home and
holds my hand the whole way. Love
takes me out at the knees in the
best way, in the best way, in the very
best way at first. Love takes its time
in coming, takes it even more in going.

Love takes.

Love takes.

(But that's to say nothing of what love gives.)

I Will

You hold my hand so
lightly, so loosely, and
I need for you to know—

I don't want to slip
away, but I could. I
might.

I will.

The Only One

I think we are reaching the point where
I can no longer say you are breaking
my heart. I think we are reaching the
point where the only one breaking it

is me.

Yours Will

When I write my version
of our ending, it will never read:

and then I gave up.

Yours will.

I Cannot

I have not given up on you.

But the world keeps on
turning, and I cannot
stop it.

Love Doesn't

Love doesn't hurt.

The things we do in its name can.

The absence of it does.

The beauty of it may
in some exquisite way.

But love

doesn't

hurt.

KRISTINA MAHR

The Twenty-Ninth of February

I have loved you on
the fourteenth of October,
the twelfth of May,
the thirty-first of December.

I have loved you on
the fifth of September,
the thirtieth of March,
the twenty-third of November.

Today is the day,
the only day,
the one day I've never loved you.

(Or it was.)

I Know

I know that I shake. I know that I
say I don't want to talk about the
things that scare me, that I stop
just short of covering my ears when
you try. I know that you think that I
deserve more, and I know that you
know how much I hate when you
say so. I know that I spend too much
time staring my worries into ceiling
fans instead of telling them to you.

I know that I shake.

But I promise, if you lean on me, I
will never let you fall.

Bad Timing

Just as I let go
of all my fears,
you let go
of me.

I Lean

Some nights I put my
back into it. I lean, I
lean, I *lean* into missing
you. It is hard not to
know where you are.
It is hard not to know
how you are. It is

hell

not to be sure I know

who you are.

I put my back into it, yes,
I put my back into it.

But I also put
my heart into it.

I Wish I Could

I did not decide
to love you, and
I cannot decide
not to.

Which Is Worse

I don't
know which
is worse:

that you ask
too much of me,

or that
I give it to you.

So Slowly

I am not running away, no, I am
walking so slowly, so slowly, that
I swear that I would stop if you
so much as

looked at me.

(No) Good

You are a good man.

You were just no good
at loving me.

Something Different

It was brave, I think, when you and I
were the only ones that still believed
in us. It is something different now
that it's only
me.

Cracking

I walk out to the center of
this frozen pond, my heart
in my outstretched palm,
and oh, I hear it cracking,
oh, I hear it cracking, oh,
I am

asking you

to love me.

Still

If it looks like love,
walks like love, talks
like love, but leaves——

it was still love.
it was still love.
it was still love.

Darker

They say the night is always
darkest before the dawn, so
each night, I wait for the
dawn, only to discover that

it can get

darker.

Every Time

I miss you every time a phone rings. a
door opens. someone says my name.
someone says your name. the sun rises.
the sun sets. the moon is full. the moon
is new. someone is laughing. someone
is crying. something changes. something
doesn't. the world turns. time passes.
my heart beats.

One of Them

I imagined whole lives
for us, I imagined whole
lives for us.

Yes, this was one of them.

It wasn't the one I hoped for.

Let It Be Fondly

If you think of me, let it be
fondly. My heart is still trying
to scrub your graffitied name
from its walls, so if you think of
me, let it be fondly. My skin
is still trying to forget your
hands, so if you think of me,
let it be fondly. My future is
still trying to untangle itself
from yours, so if you think of
me, let it be fondly.

Let it be fondly, let it
be fondly, let it be

with regret.

Plummeting

They say time heals all
wounds, but time is a drop
of rain and I'm a wildfire. It's
a band-aid and I've been
gutted. It's paper wings
and I am plummeting.

It's an *I'm sorry.*

It's an *I didn't mean to hurt you.*

It's an *I wish I could be what you need.*

Maybe it's helping.

But not enough.

It Doesn't Matter

It doesn't matter that it's mid-March;
snow falls. It doesn't matter that snow
falls; it's mid-March.

It doesn't matter that I still love you;
you're gone. It doesn't matter that you're
gone; I still love you.

What Am I Even Losing

You're not here, so what
am I even losing, what am
I even losing.

(Hope.)

Hello, Love

I leave a message after the tone, I say,
hello, love, I say, *hello, love, I was just
calling to say, how could you?* I talk until
time runs out and then it asks me if I'd
like to re-record the message and I say,
yes, of course I say, yes. This time I say,
hello, love, I say, *hello, love, I was just
calling to say, why would you?* And I
talk some more, I talk some more, didn't
you know, I have a lot to say. But time
runs out again and it asks me again and
I say yes again, of course I say yes again.
And this time I take a deep breath,
third time's the charm, I say, *hello,
love*, I say, *hello, love.*

I was just calling to say

I miss you.

I Know That I Can

I know that I can, of course
I know that I can.

But I don't want
to have to.

Beside Him

I would have

followed you

to the ends
of the earth.

But now I
walk there

beside him.

But For the Rain

But for the rain I might never have met
you. But for the rain I might never have
loved you. But for the rain I might never
have lost you. And still, I thank the rain;
I would not have liked to live in a world
where I never knew your name.

A Few Notes on Hope

The human heart is composed of
seventy-three percent water and
hope floats like boats like buoys
like empty bottles. Bottles start
out empty and float. Fill up and
sink, sink, sink. Get emptied back
out and float. Hope starts out full
and floats. Gets emptied out and
sinks, sinks, sinks. What is the other
twenty-seven percent of the human
heart and can you tell me if love is
soluble. Is there something in me pulling
up water. Pulling up water and making
rain clouds. Making rain clouds and
getting heavy. Getting heavy and
letting hope fall.

Letting hope fall like thunderclaps.

Before it fills back up

    and

        floats.

On Both of Us

Fool me once, shame on you,
fool me twice, shame on me,
no, you know what—

shame on both of us.

Ever

A thousand

miles away,

but you

are ever

beneath my

sky, and oh,

I am ever

beneath

yours.

Like So

So you love him, so you love him in
this big way, this earthquake way, this
shudder and shift and fall way, so you
love him, so you love him like mad,
like madness, like maddening, like crazy-
making, hazy-making, dizzying, so you
love him like spring, like blooming things,
like the whole wide world is waking back up
again all because you love him, because you
love him with all you have, with a little bit
more than all you have, with everything you
hope to have, want to have, swear up and
down you have to have, so you love him.

You love him like so.

How beautiful, you love him like so.

In a Language that Doesn't Have the Word Love

In a language that doesn't have the word 'love,'
I am still afraid. I am the first to pull my hand
free. I say, "I'll be fine," and I don't mean it. I say,
"it's better this way," and how could I possibly
mean it. In this language, you don't know that I
am waiting for you to hold onto my hand more
tightly. In this language, you don't know that
"I'll be fine" means "please don't leave me." In this
language, you don't know that "it's better
this way" means "I don't know how to be happy
without you." In this language, you don't know
that I am bluster and stomp and so much fear
I'm drowning in it, I'm drowning us both in it.

None of this means love.

All of this means love.

How Much

If I don't say
your name anymore,
it isn't because
I don't love you.

Oh, it's because of
how much I
still do.

With Patience

Sometimes I fight
for you with patience,
and oh, you should know,
it is the heaviest
weapon
I wield.

Let Love In

Let Love in. Even if it
comes in hand in hand
with Fear, let Love in.
Bravery is already hiding
somewhere inside, ready
if you need it even if you
don't see it, so let Love
in. Maybe it doesn't know
how to leave without
letting Hurt slip in as it
goes out, and maybe Hurt
stays far too long, far too
long, but it won't stay
forever, and someday Love
will.

You just have to
keep letting
it in.

The Only Difference

Sometimes
the only difference
between everything
and nothing
is hope.

Him

I have made a map of my heart from
years of wandering through it without
so much as a flashlight, from years of
running into walls and falling off cliffs,
from years of drowning inside of it, climbing
out of pits inside of it, I have made a map
of my heart, I have made a map of
my heart, you see, and—

around this corner, you'll find him.

through this canyon, you'll find him.

over this river, on top of these
peaks, deep in these valleys—

you'll   find   him.

In This One

In this one, I love you like gunpowder. It isn't
anything without a spark, and so it isn't anything.
In this one, we are no good for each other. We
are wounds that never graduate to scars
because we can't stop picking at them. In this
one, everyone tells me to let go. They don't see
how far the drop is. In this one, you stop calling
and you never tell me why.

In this one, I don't miss you.

(In this one, it turns out, I lie.)

It Thinks It

My brain is sorry when it gently
takes the reins back from my
heart. It is sorry, and it does not
say I told you so.

But it thinks it.

I Hope, I Hope, I Hope

My name is common enough that
you must hear it from time to
time, and oh, I hope, I hope, I
hope, each time, it breaks

your little

heart.

Brave

Look at you, a believing thing, I don't
know what to call you. Faithful? A fool,
naïve, lonely? Wanting? Wide-eyed,
gullible, trusting? I don't know what
to call you. Hopeful? Shall I call you
hopeful? Shall I call you still a fool?
A hopeful fool of foolish hopes, I think
I shall call you

brave.

Supernovas

Stars die so beautifully, exploding
into supernovas, outshining
every other star within the
universe before fading into
something small and dark.

And anyway, I loved you.

I loved you.

I loved you.

At You

I have braced for
enough falls to know
that seeing it coming
does not prevent it
from hurting.

And so now, instead of
looking down, I look
at you.

This Is Not Benevolence

What can I do with this love. I throw
fistfuls out my window like a princess
in a parade but this is not benevolence
no this is not benevolence this is
desperation. Please take it please take
it away far away please take it far away.
I have so much and he does not want
it and it is rotting here inside of me. Gather
it in your arms and make a bouquet for him
or her tonight. Take it home take it away give
it to someone who'll want it treasure it
keep it give it to someone who'll keep it.

I have so much and he does not want it.

I am so much and he does not want me.

Hard to Love

You think you are

hard to love, but,

in my experience,

you are hard

to stop loving.

Howl

I thought it would be easier
once everyone stopped asking
about you, but now all I want to
do is pull out my chair and stand
up on it and howl your name

at the top of

my lungs.

The Sky

The sky is falling and I
love you. There is plaster
in my hair and I love you.
Stars on my cheeks and I
love you. Clouds in my lungs
and I love you. Airplanes
in my eyes and I love you.
Birds in my ears and I love
you. The moon in my hands
and I love you. The sun on my
tongue and I love you.

The world stops turning but
you spin me and above us
I see something we will
someday call
the sky.

Fiction

You know, I could pick up my pen and
write you still in love with me.

But it would hurt to have to call it fiction.

Lifeboats

Maybe the
truth is I
hold onto you
so tightly
because I'm afraid
there aren't
any more lifeboats
coming,
and oh,
I am
so tired
of treading
water.

Living

I spent a whole summer wearing
a friendship bracelet on my left
wrist, tied so tight the only way
it was coming off was with scissors.
But I didn't want to cut it, no, it
was beautiful and given to me
and I didn't want to cut it.

It faded, you know. One day I
looked down and the reds were
pink and the blues were grey and
still I couldn't cut it.

I never could cut it.

But one day it wore through and
fell off somewhere, lost, and if it
took me a while to notice—

it was because I was too busy living.

Yours

Just because
you break something
doesn't mean it isn't

still

yours.

Pieces

Two is made up of two ones,
but what is one made up of?

No, I know, pieces.

So many, so many
pieces.

Maybe I'm Wrong

The birds are all singing, and they're
singing like they don't know. Probably
they don't. Probably their little pounding
hearts beneath their little fluttering wings
could not handle the knowing.

Or maybe I'm wrong, it could be
I'm wrong.

Maybe they know and they

sing anyway.

Sometimes I Dream Us

Sometimes I dream us / close my eyes and
see us / you have unopened hands and I
say all my unsaid words / we break bones
to set them right / you call me honey and I
call you mine / I write about roses / about
hummingbirds / about you / but not like
this / in there it's not a dream / in there
my eyes are open / you have to go / I
know you have to go / but in there you
come back / in here you haven't yet /
what a hopeful word is yet / what a
desperate word is yet / frayed / knotted /
frayed / reknotted / sometimes I dream us /
close my eyes and see us / open them and wonder

when the sun came up.

But I Don't

Didn't you know,
I could say goodbye
in fifteen different
languages.

But I don't.

Catch Me

They say that timing's a bitch, and
maybe they're right. Maybe I will always
love you too much in all the wrong
moments, and maybe you will never
love me enough in all the right ones.
Maybe I will always turn to look at
you just after you've turned away.
We made a game of it, in your truck,
seeing who could catch the other
looking, and

I am looking.

I am looking.

Catch me, I am looking.

I Do

You may not choose me,
but I do.

We Could've

You have always had walkaway
feet, and I have always been more
want than reason. We have both
failed us. Dropped us, cracked
us, forgotten us in the backs of
our closets for so many so many
years. I wonder if we still work.
If we took us out, dusted us off,
tried really tried would we still
work. You know, I miss us. I miss
our tangled hands and the promises
we swore to God we'd keep.

Oh perhaps we would've.

More than anything, I miss the way
we both believed we could've.

I Don't Tiptoe

I press my heels into the goddamn
ground now, I let my footsteps echo,
I don't tiptoe, no, I don't tiptoe, and
if things fall, I don't blame myself
for walking too loudly.

No, I blame whoever let it fall.

I blame whoever

didn't

catch it.

The Sun and the Moon

Someday I will
love the sun
the same as I
love the moon.

If only she, too,
would bring
me you.

An Ocean

I am falling
out of love
with you, I am.

It just takes
some time
to drain
an ocean.

Duct Tape

Hope is the duct tape
holding my heart together
until love comes to seal
all the cracks.

All the Wrong Lessons

Love sits heavy at the bottom of my heart.

A skipped stone can't stay skipping forever.
Birds can't stay in flight forever. You have
to pull the ripcord on the parachute, you
can't just fall forever.

There is no such thing as forever. Nothing comes
that cannot go. That will not go. That will have the
choice but choose not to go.

I think I learned all the wrong lessons
from loving you.

All the Places

Some nights my body
hurts in all the places
you're not touching it—

the same way my heart
hurts in all the places
you didn't want it.

I Wish You Would Go

I wish you would go / so that the cat would
choose my lap again / and the toilet seat
would never be left up / I wish you would
go / so that I could blast my music at full
volume at 7am / and nobody would ask me
questions while I try to write / I wish you
would go / so that I could watch romantic
comedies / and nobody would hog all the
sheets / but more than anything / I wish you
would go / so that I wouldn't dread you going /
and so that you couldn't see / how badly I wish

you wouldn't

go.

I Can't

I say I can't
move on from
you but
I know I mean
I won't.

And you, you know
a thing or two
about saying
can't
when you
mean won't.

Let's Say

Let's say my heart is yours. Let's say
it always has been, always will be. Let's
say I don't want it back, don't know how
to take it back. Let's say, oh, let's say
you want it. Let's say you want it.

Let's say, let's just say you think you'd
like to keep it.

Let's say you'll love me forever.

Let's say it enough times that I'll
believe it.

That Was Me

I'm sorry, I know
you never asked
to be loved this much.

No, I forgot,
that was

me.

This Time

This time I am not coy. I don't shield
my words with my arm. I don't write small.
I don't pretend it's about somebody else,
anybody else, I don't say *I have no idea
where all these words came from.* I write
your name at the top of it. I put it in
an envelope addressed to you. I drop
it in the mailbox. I wave to the mailman
as he takes it away, I don't chase
him down and ask for it back.

This time I am not coy?

I mean this time I am not afraid.

Eighth Wonder

Sometimes you'd look at me like
I was the eighth wonder of the
world, and all I wanted
was to be somewhere
you wouldn't leave.

The World

The world is probably always
going to need you more
than I do.

But oh, it cannot hold you.

It cannot hold you.

You Were Why

You used to sing
me lullabies
on nights I couldn't
sleep

and now you're gone
but that's okay
because I've realized

you were why
I couldn't sleep.

Cannot Stand

There was a time
I could not stand
to lose you.

Now I find
I cannot stand
to love you.

The Question

The question is not
how many times
will you break
my heart.

The question is
how many times
will I let you.

Lost

I lost myself in your
eyes, and I have not
found myself since.

From the Ground

We grow from the ground. Each step
forward is a rending of roots. I have
heard you say goodbye more times
than I've heard you say my name.
You come back, isn't that something,
say it's something, say *something*.
I have no torn roots. I am where you
left me, tangled in cracked sidewalk
cement, my own worst enemy. I grow
in the shadow of my own heartbreak,
and it is bigger than I am, so I don't
grow at all. You have torn every root
that grew you, and look how you tower.

Somewhere, you say I should've
known better.

Here, I wonder what I would've
become in the sunlight.

Twenty-Six Letters

When you broke my heart, twenty-six
letters fell out through the cracks in it,
and no matter how many times and ways
I arrange and rearrange them—

oh they don't bring you back.

oh they have tried and
they don't bring you back.

No Hitch, No Falter

It's getting easier every day
not to be with you.

Did you hear that?

No hitch, no falter, you
couldn't even tell it was
a lie.

(I learned from the best.)

Just This Once

I am asking you
to choose me.

To, just this once,
see the door and
choose me.

I Wouldn't

What would I do differently
if I didn't love you anymore?

Oh, I wouldn't be writing this poem.

I wouldn't have written those poems.

I wouldn't keep writing these poems.

I'm Sorry

I'm sorry that I could not
take you with me without
leaving myself behind.

Good Luck

I gave love a
compass and a map
and believed it would
find its way.

You blindfolded
it and spun it
in circles three
times and said

good luck.

How to Draw Love

1. you over there
2. me over here
3. your heart in my hand
4. my heart in your hand
5. circle all the space between us
6. draw an arrow to it
7. (don't call it emptiness)
8. (don't call it loneliness)
9. wish it was smaller, but still—
10. call it love.

Right or Wrong

You love me
all wrong, but
you love me.

Maybe there is no
right or wrong
in this.

I Will Hope

I will not slam this door,
but I will close it, and
I will not lock this door,
but I will lean against it, and
I will not wait for you to come back,
but I will hope you do.

Oh I will hope you do.

Even If

I was born to love you.

Even if I was also born
to lose you.

As Long As

I'm sure some star somewhere
was born the night I fell in love
with you, and I will love you
as long as
it shines.

Rain, the Ocean, and You

I woke up thinking about rain.

The sun is shining, though, birds
chirping, high of 72, but
I woke up thinking about rain.

I woke up thinking about the ocean.

I'm hundreds of miles away, though, dry land
far as the eye can see, no trips booked, but
I woke up thinking about the ocean.

I woke up thinking about you.

The sun is shining, though.

I'm hundreds of miles away.

But I woke up thinking about you.

A Chance

I will keep putting my heart
on the line for as long as
there's a chance that,
one of these times,
you'll want it.

Didn't It

He says he loves me, can you
believe it? Can you? Do you?
Do I? Should I? He says he
always will, isn't that something?
Isn't it? Is it? Something good,
something beautiful, something
true? He says we're meant to be,
and he says he'll never leave me.

Doesn't that sound perfect?

Doesn't it?

Doesn't it?

Didn't it?

The Letter I Didn't Send

In the letter I didn't send, I wrote
I wish I'd never met you. (I didn't
send it 'cause it isn't true.) I cursed
your name backward and forward,
pretending it isn't my favorite sound.
I was rage and hate and condescension
which stretched but did not fully cover
the pain and love and incomprehension.
I didn't say I love you, but I didn't say I
don't, because even in writing I don't lie
that well, and I wrote it in the rain, which
is why some parts look splattered.

In the letter I did send, I wrote
this is for the best.

(I guess I still sent something that isn't true.)

The Least

I'm afraid that this
will be the least I ever
love you.

Just Not Ours

And I never stopped loving you

is a happy ending

in so many stories—

just not

ours.

Distance

It is hard to shout love
across so great a distance
and still try to make it
soft.

& I Live

I close my eyes to here.
I cover my ears to now.

& I live in the past
where you still love me.

& I live in the future
where maybe
you'll love me again.

Mercy

They tell me to
set fire
to everything
he ever
touched.

And in my chest,
my heart begs for
mercy.

Bye

I am getting better at
the bye part. But there is
still no chance
of me finding
any good
in it.

A Scratch

My love for you did not leave or lessen
when my heart broke. It did not fall out,
though I can see why you might think
it did, cracks that size, holes that wide.
It broke into all of its pieces, but I still
have it in here, sharp-edged and sorry.
It clings to the rim of each heartbeat;
gets brave and picks fights after midnight.

What does a broken record play
when you set it on the turntable?

I love and a scratch and a *you.*

And never an

I love you, too.

I Live Around It

I've never stopped loving
anyone I've really loved
before; they just leave and I
live around it.

Alone

I tell myself
if we're both alone
then neither of us
is alone.

But it doesn't keep
me warm.

Enough

Love has always been enough.

It's us that haven't been.

Apart

I thought nothing
could keep us
apart.

And if something
did, I didn't think
it would be you.

I Hope Anyway

If I was a different person, I might
believe that you still love me.

I'm not but I
hope anyway.

I Learned

I learned the hard way
that you are not a place
where people lean.

You are a place
where people fall.

You are a place
where people

break.

Sunset

I wish it was
the beauty of the sunset
that reminded me of you,
but no, it's the way
it takes all the light with it
when it goes.

Penny for Your Thoughts

Penny for your thoughts? Make it
a dime. A dollar. A hundred. A
thousand. They say talk is cheap,
but it doesn't have to be. Name
your price.

It can't be as high
as the cost of your silence.

The Kindest Thing

The kindest thing
you could ever give me
is answers.

I guess the kindest thing
I could ever give you
is to try to understand
without them.

Let's Forget

Let's forget for a little while that I
loved you. That you had your fingers
crossed behind your back when you
said you loved me too. That I wasn't
enough for you to stay. That you
weren't strong enough to stay. That I
have cried the Pacific over you. That
you pretended not to see its crashing
waves. That every star we wished
upon is dead already. That every wish
we wished was a promise we could've
made instead.

Let's forget for a little while
that I loved you.

Let's forget for a little while
that I said *loved* instead of
love.

As It Stands

I have loved you long enough.

I would have loved you longer,
but as it stands—

I have loved you long enough.

A Fighter's Heart

I have a fighter's heart— black
and blue and scarred and bloodied
and half lost to the mats and half
lost to him and too soft for this
life and no clue when to quit and
forever and ever and ever out
searching for someone who'll

fight back.

Grasping

Sometimes I'm looking and I can't
find the right words to tell you I'm
lost without you. It's like grasping
at thin air for something that might
have a chance of saving you. All
the words I think might be the right
ones are just out of reach, just
across the country, just over the
ocean, just possibly in the part
of my heart you still have.

I wish you were here.

I would say it better if you were.

Liars

I keep dreaming
that you come back
and say you're sorry
and I say it's okay.

I keep dreaming
that we're both liars.

Never Meant

sunscreen sticky and / freshly freckled / the
backs of my eyelids glow gold / giving you
the backdrop of an Apollo / or an Icarus / from
which to haunt me / forgetting you is a fool's
errand / something is crawling across my skin /
light like fingertips / I should swat it away / but
in this gold glow / it's possible it's you / anything
is possible here / even the impossible / Apollo
never meant / to fall in love with Daphne / Icarus
never meant / to fly into the sun / you say you
never meant / to hurt me.

in another hour / the tide will wash up over
me / and I will say / I never meant to stay so long.

but as it grows higher / I still won't go.

Kickstand

In this one, I want you to be the kickstand,
holding me up when I tire. The wheels are
my dreams, ever spinning, carrying me
on, and I am still me, pedaling toward
something I can't always see clearly. These
poems are the ringing bell that warns people
I am on my way. Fear is my brakes, too close
at hand.

In this one, I want you to be the kickstand,
but you are the gravel beneath my wheels,
the stifling heat of the day, the strong wind
that sends me sideways.

In this one, you're something to be

overcome.

Cruel

I thought maybe this would
all be easier if I hated you. I
asked you once to say something
cruel so I might try it, but instead,
you said nothing at all.

You are better at this than I expected.

Better Off

You say that I'd
be better off
without you, and
I wonder if you think
a heart works better
when it's broken.

Drowning

I thought that letting go of
you meant letting go of the
only thing keeping me from
drowning.

It turns out letting go of
you meant letting go of the
only thing keeping me

drowning.

Too Tightly

Hurt has never been content riding
shotgun. It sits on my lap, curled up
against my chest, pushing against
my lungs until I can't breathe. It
forces my chin up so all I see is the
rearview mirror. It whispers in my
ear the whole way, except for every
now and then when it shouts, and it
sings along to all the sad songs.

It tells me to turn around.

It tells me I'm going the wrong way.

And when we get home, it lies in bed
beside me and holds

my hand

too tightly.

To

They all call me a
runner and they
aren't wrong. I
always wondered
what I was running
from, but then I
met you and realized—

I was running to.

Regrets

I know that I am
one of your regrets
though I wish I knew

if it was because
you ever left me

or because
you ever loved me.

Sad Little Poems

I could write sonnets
to the way that
I love you.

But instead I write
these sad little poems
to the way that
you don't care.

KRISTINA MAHR

In a World Where Time Runs Backward

I am sad for three years before I meet him. I get off the plane and walk straight into the airport bathroom to cry for twenty minutes. I call him and he doesn't answer. He is waiting outside, and I don't want to hug him but I know I'll regret it if I don't. We climb into his truck and he says he's sorry. We drive home and he says he doesn't love me anymore, but then I lean my head upon his shoulder, and it is warm and I am happy. I am happy. I am happy. Months pass. We are drunk at a bar and I think he's the most beautiful thing I've ever seen. The next morning I've forgotten him. I am not sad but I am not happy. I am not happy. I am not happy.

I have never been in love.

I have never been loved.

222

CONTENTS

ACKNOWLEDGMENTS

I am who I am, both as a person and as a writer, because of the people I love, the people who love me, the people I loved, and the people who loved me. I am grateful for all of them.

And I am grateful for you, for holding these words in your hands. It helps so much to share their weight.

ABOUT THE AUTHOR

Kristina Mahr devotes her days to numbers and her nights
to words. She works full-time as an accountant in the
suburbs of Chicago, but her true passion is writing. In her
spare time, she enjoys spending time with her family,
friends, and small herd of rescue animals, as well as waking
up at the crack of dawn every weekend to watch the
Premier League.

You can find more information about her other poetry
collections, as well as her fiction novels, on her website at:

www.kristinamahr.com

Made in the USA
Coppell, TX
29 March 2023

14933565R00134